I0201401

The Sherlock Holmes Drama Series
Volume One

by Sir Arthur Conan Doyle
Dramatisation by Michael Mandeville

A Study in Scarlet
The Illustrious Client
The Naval Treaty
The Sussex Vampire
The Norwood Builder

Published by Cambridge Digital

Copyright © 2011 Cambridge Digital
All rights reserved.

The Sherlock Holmes Drama Series
Volume One

Contents

The Sherlock Holmes Drama Series
Volume One
by Sir Arthur Conan Doyle
Dramatisation by Michael Mandeville

ISBN 978-1-906118-05-1

A Study in Scarlet
The Illustrious Client
The Naval Treaty
The Sussex Vampire

The characters of Sir Arthur Conan Doyle, are used here by kind permission of Jonathan Clowes Ltd., on behalf of Andrea Plunket, Administrator of the Conan Doyle Copyrights.

Series Editor: Will Burrows
Cover image: Tim Edwards

Published by Cambridge Digital
St Johns Innovation Centre
Cowley Road
Cambridge
CB4 0WS
www.cambridgedigital.com
hello@cambridgedigital.com

Copyright © 2011 Cambridge Digital
All rights reserved.

The Sherlock Holmes Drama Series

The Sherlock Holmes Drama Series is a collection of dramatisations of Conan Doyle's Sherlock Holmes stories, written for performance times of ten to fifteen minutes. Longer stories have been divided into sections to maintain this.

The language remains close to the original stories, and where it is simplified and condensed, reflects the culture and style of the originals.

Visit the website

The plays have been written with schools and learners of English in mind, and performance notes, follow-up exercises and learning materials are available at:

www.cambridgedigital.com/sherlockholmes

Performance rights

The plays may be performed in schools without permission, but please notify us that you intend to use them by emailing **drwatson@cambridgedigital.com**. No grant of copyright is given or implied by this authority.

All other rights are reserved; performance licences must be obtained for all other public performances. Please email **drwatson@cambridgedigital.com** or write to:

Dr Watson
Cambridge Digital
St John's Innovation Centre
Cowley Road
Cambridge
CB4 0WS

Copyright

The characters of Sir Arthur Conan Doyle, are used here by kind permission of Jonathan Clowes Ltd., on behalf of Andrea Plunket, Administrator of the Conan Doyle Copyrights. All other copyrights are owned by Cambridge Digital.

A Study in Scarlet

by Sir Arthur Conan Doyle
Dramatisation by Michael Mandeville

PART ONE

CAST:
Dr John H. Watson
Dr Stamford, a colleague
Mr Sherlock Holmes
A retired Sergeant of Marines

Dr Watson: (narration) As this is the first account of my extraordinary experiences with an extraordinary man, perhaps I should begin by introducing myself. My name is John Henry Watson. I was born in London, in 1878. I took my degree in medicine at the University there, after which I joined the British Army as a surgeon. I was transferred straight away to India, where the Second Afghan War had broken out, and on arrival, attached to the Berkshire Regiment and sent to Kandahar. Travel and adventure was my object: it was not, however, my destiny; for there, at our very first engagement, the ill-fated battle of Maiwand, I was struck in the shoulder by a jezail bullet. It shattered the bone; and so completely that, of no further service to the Army, I was invalided back to England. Thus, only 18 months after leaving, I returned to where I started, but with ruined health, an inadequate pension, no family or prospects - and nowhere to live.

This last was the most pressing of my problems; and I was wondering what to do about it when, one morning on a busy London Street, I felt a tap on my shoulder.

(**Scene:** a busy London street in 1880)
Dr Stamford: Excuse me, it is Dr Watson, isn't it?
Dr Watson: Yes! Who... why - it's young Stamford! - my assistant at the Hospital - what, five years ago?
Dr Stamford: That's right, sir: though I must admit, I hardly recognised you. You're so thin and sunburned!
Dr Watson: Oh, that's Army service. What about you?
Dr Stamford: Still at the Hospital. I take my degree this year.
Dr Watson: Splendid!

Dr Stamford: What are you doing now? Are you busy?

Dr Watson: (laughs) Actually, I'm looking for a place to live. Digs, you know.

Dr Stamford: I meant - have you time for a drink?

Dr Watson: Oh - always time for that!

Dr Stamford: Though funnily enough I was talking to someone else this morning about that very thing... (fade out)

(**Scene:** interior of public house)

Dr Stamford: (continuing)... actually, he's found it. Nice digs, he says but too big and too expensive for him alone.

Dr Watson: Hmmm. Sharing digs, eh. I never thought of that. What's he like?

Dr Stamford: Pleasant fellow, good family...

Dr Watson: What does he do?

Dr Stamford: He's at the Hospital as well. Laboratory: anatomy, physiology, pathology. Nothing systematic, though.

Dr Watson: Perhaps he's a student.

Dr Stamford: Good Lord, no.

Dr Watson: Did you never ask him?

Dr Stamford: He's... not the kind of fellow one asks that kind of question.

Dr Watson: I'd like to meet him, anyway. Can you arrange it?

Dr Stamford: With pleasure!

Dr Watson: By the way - what's his name?

Dr Stamford: His name is... Sherlock Holmes.

(**Scene:** University quadrangle)

Dr Stamford: Well, here's the Laboratory: I'll take you in and introduce you. But before I do you must promise me one thing.

Dr Watson: What's that?

Dr Stamford: That you won't blame me if you don't get on with him.

Dr Watson: Good Heavens, no! It was my idea! But why do you think I won't get on with him?

Dr Stamford: Well, he's a little odd - for my taste a bit too scientific - rather cold-blooded, in fact.

Dr Watson: (laughs) Pathology is a cold-blooded sort of science, you know, dead bodies and all that.

Dr Stamford: Which he beats with a stick?

Dr Watson: (startled) What?

Dr Stamford: I've seen him do it. "To verify how far bruises can be inflicted after death," he explained. He appears to have a passion for definite and exact knowledge.

Dr Watson: (doubtful) Hmmm - that's commendable enough...
Dr Stamford: So he beats bodies?
Dr Watson: (coughs) Extraordinary...
Dr Stamford: Still interested?
Dr Watson: (making up his mind) Yes – why not!

(**Scene:** Hospital Laboratory - echoes)
Dr Stamford: Ah - there you are, Holmes. I'd like to introduce you to a friend of mine. Dr John Watson - Sherlock Holmes.
Dr Watson: How do you do.
Holmes: (friendly) How do you do. You've been in Afghanistan, I see. Wounded at the battle of Maiwand - jezail bullet through the right shoulder. Never mind - welcome back to England.
Dr Watson: I... ah... well... hmmm... er...
Dr Stamford: Watson's an old friend of mine, Holmes; and guess what? He's looking for someone to share digs with!
Holmes: Is he, by Jove! You told him I'd found some?
Dr Stamford: Yes.
Holmes: It's a very nice apartment, first floor, right on the street. Two bedrooms, large sitting-room, reasonable rent and most convenient.
Dr Watson: Where is it?
Holmes: (laughs) Oh - stupid of me. It's at the top end of Baker Street. Number 221b. (fade out)

Dr Watson: (narration) We moved in the next day, and settled down. Despite Stamford's fears, I did not find Holmes difficult to live with; on the contrary, he was quiet, tidy and considerate - and played the violin beautifully. With time I learned of other things; but one I could not discover: the nature of his work. He rose early and was back late. He had visitors; two regular ones, a sallow, rat-faced little man, and a big, blond one; and all sorts of others, mostly, it seemed, from the lower classes. On these occasions he would beg me for the use of the sitting-room, and I would retire to my bedroom. No, I couldn't ask him outright what he did: rules were rather strict about such things, especially then. So I had to content myself with drawing up a list of what I knew of him, and trying to puzzle out an answer. It started with a description.

Sherlock Holmes: age about 30: height, somewhat above six feet, but so extremely lean as to appear taller. A long, thin face, square jaw, piercing grey eyes, dark hair. Contrary to fashion, no beard or moustache. Long, powerful, sensitive hands. His knowledge and abilities are strange. He knows nothing of philosophy, literature or

politics, yet a great deal about law, physics and chemistry, and what's in the newspapers. Is an expert swordsman, pistol-shot and boxer, to judge by the trophies he has won. Plays the violin unusually well; and has the most comprehensive knowledge about crime. He appears to know everything, to the last, most gory detail, about every murder, suicide, robbery, arson, assault and rape that has ever been committed!

His accomplishments, then, are eccentric, and give no clue as to his occupation. Even his music is eccentric: for hours he will sit his violin across his knees, scraping away tunelessly and staring into space; but at the end, sensing my discomfort, he will lift it to his chin and treat me to such an excellent selection of Schubert, Mendelssohn and Beethoven, that I forgive him.

Thus, after several weeks of silent and frustrated speculation, I was as distant from the truth as even. Until a certain morning. We were standing at the window, looking down into the street...

(**Scene:** Holmes' rooms, 221b Baker Street)
Dr Watson: I say, look at that fellow over there, with the letter. Do think he's lost?
Holmes: You mean the retired sergeant of Marines? Yes, he doesn't know his way around.
Dr Watson: How do you know he's an ex-sergeant of Marines?
Holmes: Oh, look - he's coming here! I wonder if it's me he wants. (Sound of boots on stairs outside - ring at bell - door opens)
Sergeant: (gruffly) Letter for Mr Sherlock Holmes.
Holmes: That is I. Thank you.
Sergeant: Any reply, sir?
Dr Watson: One moment, please. You don't look like a messenger. What's your occupation?
Sergeant: I'm a commissionaire, sir. My uniform's away for cleaning.
Dr Watson: And before that?
Sergeant: Sergeant, sir: Royal Marine Light Infantry.
Holmes: Thank you, sergeant. No reply.
Sergeant: Very good, sir. (Door closes)
Dr Watson: (after a pause) Holmes?
Holmes: Yes?
Dr Watson: How did you know that?
Holmes: Know what?
Dr Watson: That that man was an ex-sergeant of Marines?

Holmes: It's part of my work.

Dr Watson: What - knowing people's occupation, just by looking at them.

Holmes: Yes.

Dr Watson: Is that how you knew I came from Afghanistan, and was at Maiwand?

Holmes: Yes.

Dr Watson: How did you know that?

Holmes: Oh, very simple. Stamford said you were a doctor, yet you wore your hand-kerchief in your sleeve as many Army people do: therefore you were an Army doc-tor. You were deeply sunburned, so you must have been in the tropics. You had been wounded in the right shoulder: I felt the bone was damaged the moment I shook hands with you. Only a jezail bullet can do that. The last action where the British suffered casualties which included doctors and jezail bullets, was at Mai-wand.

Dr Watson: (much impressed) Why, that's wonderful!

Holmes: Commonplace.

Dr Watson: Ahem. And the sergeant?

Holmes: An anchor tattooed on the back of his hand means the sea, yet he wears regulation side-whiskers, which is Army. Both together mean Marines. He carries a walking-stick, but swings it as sergeants do their canes. Therefore he is - or was - a sergeant.

Dr Watson: (becoming agitated) Holmes - are you going to tell me, or must I ask you - WHAT IS YOUR WORK!

Holmes: (taken aback) My work?

Dr Watson: Yes! Who are all those people who come to see you?

Holmes: People?

Dr Watson: Those two men, for example, who were here again last night!

Holmes: Inspector Lestrade and Inspector Gregson, both of Scotland Yard.

Dr Watson: Scotland... (gulp: in disbelief) Are you... a policeman?

Holmes: No, I'm a detective - a consulting detective.

Dr Watson: What in Heaven's... what is that?

Holmes: England has a lot of government detectives - also a lot of private ones. Whenever these fellows have difficulty with their cases, or find themselves at fault, they come to me, who am usually better qualified to find the answer. Like now, for instance, in this letter. "There has been a bad business during the night at No 3, Lauriston Gardens, off the Brixton Road. The dead man is an American; but he has not been robbed and there is no indication of how he died. Can you help? Signed Inspector Gregson."

Dr Watson: (impressed) Well... Good Lord! What are you going to do?

Holmes: Go along and look, I suppose. Would you like to come?

Dr Watson: (astonished) Me?

Holmes: Well, you're a doctor. You may be useful. But you don't have to. It's entirely up to you.

Dr Watson: (A deep breath as he makes the momentous decision) All right. I'll come!

Part Two

Cast:
Mr Sherlock Holmes
Dr John Watson
Inspector Lestrade - a small and scrawny Londoner.
Inspector Gregson - a big, bluff Londoner.
Police Constable John Rance
Mrs Sawyer - an old crone.
Cab-driver - a gruff Cockney.
Wiggins - a 12-year-old street urchin.

Dr Watson: (narration) Here I was, Dr John Watson, invalided from the British Army, suddenly made assistant to a consulting detective and travelling to the scene of my first sudden death. I could hardly believe it! As we drove along, Sherlock Holmes told me a little of his work - and of the personalities involved.

(**Scene:** the interior of a horse-drawn cab: sound of hooves etc)
Holmes: The two most senior inspectors at Scotland Yard are Lestrade and Gregson, and they're on this case together.
Dr Watson: (jovial) Well, that's comforting!
Holmes: I said that they were senior - not that they were any good.
Dr Watson: Oh, aren't they?
Holmes: No - hopeless; and the fact that they're such deadly rivals isn't going to help the case much either. Ah - here's the Brixton Road.
Dr Watson: Have you formed any conclusions of your own?
Holmes: Of course not - there's no data. It's a bad mistake to theorise before you have your data. (calling) Just stop here, Cabby we'll do the rest on foot.
Cabby: Right, sir! Whoa there. (the hoof beats slow)

Dr Watson: (**narration**) Number 3, Lauriston Gardens, was an empty house, dark gloomy and foreboding. As we approached, Holmes paid great attention to the ground, studying the tracks and footmarks in the soil. One of the Inspectors met us at the door.

Insp. Gregson: Very kind of you to come, sir!

Holmes: Not at all. This is Dr Watson, my colleague. Inspector Gregson.

Dr Watson: How do you do

Insp. Gregson: How d'you do. I've left everything untouched, sir. It's just as we discovered it.

Holmes: (with asperity) Except for the herd of buffalo you allowed to pass between the front gate and the front door!

Insp. Gregson: (unabashed) That's the local police, sir - Lestrade's fault. He should have stopped 'em.

Holmes: Did you come here in a cab?

Insp. Gregson: (surprised) No, sir. - Would you like to step inside now?

Dr Watson: (**narration**) Never shall I forget that scene. The body lay upon its back in the centre of the room, its arms out flung: a man of about 45, well-dressed, powerfully built. His lower limbs were interlocked, his fists were clenched, and on his face an expression of such rage and hate as I could never have imagined. Bright blood lay everywhere about the floor, in scarlet pools and splashes: a single candle stood upon the mantelpiece. There was no other furniture: like the house, the room was bare and still. Holmes approached the body.

(**Scene:** the interior, No 3, Lauriston Gardens)

Holmes: Are you sure there's no wound, Lestrade?

Insp. Lestrade: Yes, sir. Not so far as we can see.

Then where does all this blood come from?

Insp. Lestrade: No idea, sir.

Holmes: Are there any clues at all?

Insp. Lestrade: Just this, sir. I found it underneath the body.

Holmes: Hmmm - a woman's wedding-ring.

Insp. Gregson: What does that mean, d'you think?

Insp. Lestrade: (sarcastic) It means there's been a woman here - what else!

Insp. Gregson: Not necessarily. It could mean...

Holmes: Have you searched his pockets?

Insp. Lestrade: I put it all inside his nice new hat, sir, which we found next to the body. Gold watch and chain - gold ring with initials EJD - leather card-case in name of Enoch J. Drebber, of Cleveland, Ohio, USA - and two letters, one addressed to Drebber and the other to a Joseph Stangerson.

Holmes: At what address?

Insp. Lestrade: American Exchange, in the Strand.

Holmes: And Stangerson?

Insp. Lestrade: We're making enquiries for him now.

Holmes: Who found the body?

Insp. Lestrade: Inspector Gregson can tell you about that - I hope.

Insp. Gregson: The body was discovered at one o'clock this morning by Constable Rance, who was on the beat. He saw a light in what he knew to be an empty house, investigated, and found what you see now.

Insp. Lestrade: (at a distance: triumphant) Not what you see now! Look what *I've* found!

Holmes: What is it?

Insp. Lestrade: Here - on the wall - very faint - written in blood with someone's fingertip: the letters R.A.C.H.E. Racher. See - I told you!

Insp. Gregson: Told me what?

Insp. Lestrade: There was a woman here! That's 'RACHEL'. There just wasn't enough time to finish it.

Insp. Gregson: (derisive) Oh, get on with you! That's just children, scribbling. You've got women on the brain, you have... (fade out)

Dr Watson: (narration) Leaving the two of them to squabble, Sherlock Holmes began what I came to learn and recognise as the most important aspect of his work: the scenes of crime examination. With his magnifying glass in his hand and the deepest concentration, up and down, sometimes on his knees, looking, peering, sniffing, feeling, he examined every inch of the dead body, the room, the walls, the floor, the window... After a while he stood up.

(**Scene:** return to No 3, Lauriston Gardens)

Insp. Gregson: Well, Mr Holmes?

Holmes: Well, gentlemen?

Insp. Lestrade: Did you find anything?

Holmes: What did you want to know?

Insp. Lestrade: Well, er - what's it all about?

Holmes: It's murder, gentlemen - by poison. There were two men here: one whom you see now, the other about the same age but much taller and stronger. He brought his victim here in a four-wheel cab. Anything else?

Insp. Lestrade: What about the woman? The ring?

Holmes: There was no woman. R.A.C.H.E. also spells Rache - which is German for 'revenge'.

Insp. Gregson: (laughs loudly) Revenge! Hear that, Lestrade? Where's your girlfriend now, eh? Ha ha ha!

Holmes: (undertone) Come along, Watson. First I have to send a telegram then interview Constable Rance, the man on beat... (fade out)

(**Scene:** Audley Court, Kennington Park; residence of Const. Rance)
Holmes: ... and after you'd found the body, Constable, what did you do?
PC Rance: (a heavy Cockney) I went to the front gate and blew me whistle, sir.
Holmes: Did anyone come?
Rance: Of course! My mate, P/C Murcher, an' a couple more Constables.
Holmes: Anyone else?
Rance: Only some drunk...
Holmes: A drunk!
Rance: Yeah, he were real sozzled, this one. Standin' by the front gate, singin'
and shoutin'...
Holmes: What did he look like?
Rance: Oh, big, tall chap, carryin' a whip. Proper sight he was. (laughs)
Holmes: Thank you, Constable - you've been very helpful... (fade out)

(**Scene:** 221b Baker Street: the following morning)
Holmes: The ring, Watson - the ring! That's what he came back for!
Dr Watson: Who - the man with the whip?
Holmes: Yes.
Dr Watson: You mean... he's the murderer?
Holmes: Of course.
Dr Watson: (impressed) My word...! But it doesn't say anything about the ring in
today's paper (he rustles it).
Holmes: Because they don't realise its significance. Lestrade is still looking for
his lady-friend and Gregson is looking for Stangerson. But as a matter of fact the
ring is mentioned in the paper.
Dr Watson: Where?
Holmes: Back page - Lost and Found - (paper rustles) - there!
Dr Watson: (reading) "Found, in Brixton Road last night, a plain gold wedding
ring. Apply Dr Watson, 221b Baker Street... " Hey - that's...
Holmes: Of course it is! I can't use my name - it's too well known. Here's the ring
- or one just like it. He's sure to call for it. But be careful - he may be dangerous.
Dr Watson: (horrified) What!
Holmes: Do you have a gun?
Dr Watson: I... er... yes... I think... (doorbell rings: shrilly) Holmes! Don't leave
me!
Holmes: I'll be in the next room. Call me if he kills you (door closes)
Dr Watson: Oh my good... c c c come in!
(Enter Mrs Sawyer, a quavering old crone)
Mrs Sawyer: Good morning, sir. I'm Mrs Sawyer. I've come about the ring.
Dr Watson: (gulps) The ring? Ah yes I Are you sure it's yours?

Mrs Sawyer: Not mine, sir - my daughter Sally's. She lost it in the Brixton Road last night.

Dr Watson: Is this it?

Mrs Sawyer: The Lord be thanked! Yes - that's the one! Bless you, sir

Dr Watson: Not at all. I'll see you out.

Mrs Sawyer: She'll be that pleased to see it again - she was so worried. Good day to you, sir, and thank you once again for all your kindness.

Dr Watson: A pleasure, Mrs Sawyer. Goodbye... (Door closes)

Holmes: (opening door) Hullo - still alive?

Dr Watson: (faintly) Just about...

Holmes: Good. You stay here - I'm going after that old lady...

Dr Watson: (calling) Watch out - she may be dangerous.

(**Narration**) But it was a tired and rueful Sherlock Holmes who returned some hours later - empty-handed. (Returns to previous scene) (in disbelief) Got away from you Holmes? A feeble old woman like that?

Holmes: Feeble old woman be damned! That was a young man - an actor and a very good one, too - obviously hired for the occasion. I'm afraid we're up against someone rather clever...

(He is interrupted by a banging on the door and a ringing of the door opens and there is a sudden tumult of shrill young voices)

Dr Watson: (above the noise: in amazement) Good Lord, Holmes - what's all this? A dozen dirty little ragamuffins...

Holmes: The Baker Street Irregulars, Watson. My private detective force - go everywhere, see everything... Wiggins!

Wiggins: (like an RSM) Baker Street Irregulars - 'shun! (sudden silence)

Holmes: Well, Wiggins - have you found it yet?

Wiggins: No, sir, but we ain't finished yet.

Holmes: What are you looking for?

Wiggins: Three ole shoes, sir, an' one noo 'un: initials JH on it.

Holmes: Right. Off you go then - and find them!

Wiggins: Yessir. Baker Street Irregulars - Dis – miss!

(Scamper, rush of feet, and voices fade)

Dr Watson: (astonished) Holmes! Do you know who this man is we're looking for?

Holmes: Oh yes. It's just a question of locating him, that's all.

Dr Watson: But what about Stangerson? Why doesn't he come forward?

Holmes: That is a little puzzling, certainly.

Dr Watson: Is he the man with the whip?

Holmes: He... (there is a bang on the door) Excuse me. (He opens the door) Ah - Inspector Gregson! Any news?

Insp. Gregson: Indeed I have! Congratulate me, gentlemen! I have the murderer of Enoch Drebber safely under lock and key!

Holmes: (somewhat perturbed) What! Who?

Insp. Gregson: (grandly) His name is... Arthur Charpentier!

Holmes: (laughing with relief) Well, well! Take a seat, Inspector - tell us all about it.

Insp. Gregson: (making himself comfortable) Brains, Mr Holmes - that's all it takes. Brains! You remember that the dead man's hat was new?

Holmes: Yes. Made by John Underwood and Sons, 129 Camberwell Road.

Insp. Gregson: Oh. (Coughs) You noticed, did you... Well, I had the idea they might have his address - and they did: Enoch Drebber, care of Charpentier's Boarding House, Camberwell. I went there - and it didn't take me long to find out what had happened. Drebber and Stangerson were staying together there. On the night of the murder, Drebber, who was a bit of a drunken brute, made advances to Alice Charpentier, daughter of the owner; whereon her brother, seeing this, took him outside and beat hell out of him! And he admits it!

Holmes: Does he, by Jove!

Insp. Gregson: (laughing uproariously) And to think that idiot Lestrade is still searching London for... ha ha ha!

(The doorbell rings: door opens) Why - here he is! Well, Lestrade did you manage to find your Mr Stangerson?

Insp. Lestrade: (equably) Yes, as a matter of fact I did.

Insp. Gregson: Where was he - making love to Rachel in Hyde Park? Ha ha ha!

Insp. Lestrade: I found Mr Stangerson in his hotel room this morning.

Insp. Gregson: What!

Insp. Lestrade: He had been murdered; and written in blood on the wall above his head, was the word 'Rache'.

Part Three

Cast:
Mr Sherlock Holmes
Dr John Watson
Inspector Lestrade
Inspector Gregson
Wiggins
Jefferson Hope: an American, in his forties, big and powerful.
Lucy Ferrier: an American girl aged about 7.

John Ferrier: An American, in his forties, quiet and restrained.
Brigham Young: An American, aged in his fifties, massive and compelling

Dr Watson: (narration) My first investigation with Sherlock Holmes. Enoch Drebber, an American, had been found poisoned. The obvious suspect was his secretary, Joseph Stangerson, who had disappeared; but two mornings later Inspector Lestrade of Scotland Yard called to give us some grim and unexpected news.

(**Scene:** Holmes' rooms at 221b Baker Street, London)
Insp. Lestrade: He's dead, gentlemen. Joseph Stangerson was stabbed to death in his hotel room this morning.
Holmes: (shocked) Stabbed to death?
Insp. Lestrade: ...and on the wall above his head, in his own blood, was written the word 'Rache'.
Dr Watson: Revenge, eh.
Insp. Gregson: Must be a secret Society. The Vehmgericht, or the Carbonari, or maybe the Socialists...
Holmes: Inspector Gregson here has already arrested someone else for Drebber's murder.
Insp. Lestrade: (unpleasantly) Has he. Then he'd better let him go again, hadn't he.
Insp. Gregson: (irritated) Maybe you'd better tell us what happened!
Insp. Lestrade: Happy to oblige. All it took was brains, you know.
Insp. Gregson: Hah!
Insp. Lestrade: I looked at it this way. Either Stangerson killed Drebber or he didn't. If he did then he'd be hiding somewhere, and we'd have to find him in the normal way. But suppose he didn't, and was waiting for him somewhere, not knowing he'd been killed? Where would he wait? Why - at or near the place they'd last been seen together, which, as it was a railway station, Euston, made it even more likely.
Holmes: Good thinking. Eh, Gregson?
Insp. Gregson: (offhand) Strictly routine.
Insp. Lestrade: So I started there; and found him almost straight away, at Halliday's Private Hotel. Mr Stangerson? He's upstairs in his room, they told me, so upstairs I went. (His voice changes) find then I saw it, underneath the door, trickling in a thick red river: blood.
Dr Watson: (hoarsely) Good... God!
Insp. Lestrade: He hadn't been dead long - he was still warm - still in his nightshirt. There'd been a fight - you could see that. And you could see how the mur-

derer got in: the window was open and there was a ladder up outside. But no ring this time, no motive: only 'Rache' on the wall.

Holmes: And he was stabbed, you say?

Insp. Lestrade: Yes - clean through the heart. But no sign of the weapon.

Holmes: Anything else?

Insp. Lestrade: Not much. A telegram from Cleveland, Ohio: "JH is in Europe", a book, a pipe, eighty pounds in cash, a little box containing two pills...

Holmes: What!

Insp. Lestrade: I said a little box containing...

Holmes: Do you still have it?

Insp. Lestrade: (puzzled) Yes, right here, but...

Holmes: (urgently) Watson, be a good chap and get that poor old dog of the landlady's, the one she wanted you to put to sleep yesterday.

Dr Watson: Oh, all right... (exits)

Insp. Gregson: Dog, Mr Holmes? Did you say 'dog'?

Holmes: Yes - you'll see. Now first I take one of these little pills of Stangerson's. I cut it in half and... dissolve it in a saucer of water. Then... I do the same to the other, in a separate saucer. Ah - here's Watson.

Dr Watson: (entering) I've brought the dog.

Holmes: Good - put him on the floor, (to dog) Here, boy. Drink this. There you go... (sound of dog lapping water)

Insp. Gregson: (after a short pause) Now what?

Holmes: I give him the other saucer. (To dog) Here, old fellow... poor old chap, he's so sick. Drink it up now. There... (dog laps)

Insp. Lestrade: What...!

Dr Watson: I say...!

Insp. Gregson: It's dead! Just like that! It must have been poison!

Holmes: It was. Watson - would you take the dog downstairs again?

Insp. Lestrade: But that was out of Stangerson's room! How did you know...

Insp. Gregson: (becoming angry) Come on, Mr Holmes, you're playing around with us - What's going on, eh?

Holmes: I can't tell you yet.

Insp. Lestrade: Look, whoever is responsible could be out committing other crimes.

Holmes: No, no, he won't do that.

Insp. Gregson: How do you know! He might...

Dr Watson: Excuse me, Holmes, there's someone here to see you.

Holmes: Oh - hullo, Wiggins!

Wiggins: Hullo, guv'nor! I've got that cab far you. It's waitin' downstairs.

Holmes: Oh, good. But one of the boxes is rather heavy. Would you ask the cab-man to step up and give me a hand?

Wiggins: Right away, guv'nor! (exits)

Dr Watson: You going somewhere, Holmes?

Holmes: For a few days. By the way, Inspector, have you seen this new kind of handcuff? Look how beautifully it works (click-click). You should introduce it at Scotland Yard.

Insp. Lestrade: (growls) The old kind's good enough for us - if we can find the right man to put 'em on.

(There is a knock at the door: it opens)

Cabby: Cabby, sir. You've a box you want downstairs?

Holmes: Yes - here. If you'll just take the handle...

Cabby: Here?

Holmes: Yes - use both hands, it's easier. Like this... (There is the click-click of the handcuffs and a startled shout from the cabby) Gentlemen - let me introduce you to Mr Jefferson Hope, the murderer of Enoch Drebber and Joseph Stangerson! (pandemonium)

Wiggins: (shrieks) Look out!

Insp. Gregson: Stop him!

Insp. Lestrade: Hold him!

Wiggins: He's tryin' for the window! (tremendous sound of breaking glass)

Dr Watson: My God!

Holmes: Grab his legs!

Insp. Gregson: I've got his collar!

Insp. Lestrade: Pull him back!

(There is the sound of a furious struggle. Hope, alias the Cabby, is roaring with rage; everyone else is exclaiming with excitement. Gradually the noise dies down. Everyone is panting as he speaks)

Jeff Hope: (a booming, powerful American) All right - you got me! I'll give you no more trouble. (He laughs)

Insp. Gregson: I'll say you won't! My God, what a brute!

Holmes: I think you'd better get him to the station - get those wounds treated as well. And then we'll hear what he has to say.

(**Scene:** the interrogation room at Scotland Yard)

Insp. Gregson: ... and I warn you, Jefferson Hope, that anything you say will be taken down in writing and may be used as evidence...

Jeff Hope: All right, all right. You want me to start at the beginning?

Holmes: It might be best.

Jeff Hope: It goes back a long way - 40 years to be exact, to the great alkali plain of Utah State in North America. You won't know that part of the world, gentlemen, but believe me - it ain't worth knowing. Mountains to the north and south, canyons to the east and west; and in the middle, a hundred miles of it - which must be crossed - nothing. No trees, no grass, no pools, no streams. Just... death. And if you'd been there, on a day in May in 1847, you'd have seen two people, all alone in the middle of that wide and empty plain, doin' just that: - dying. Only one of them didn't know it, while the other did...

(Fade to desert landscape, open, empty: only sound the sighing of the wind and a man breathing heavily as he trudges along) After a while the fresh voice of a little girl is heard)

Lucy: How much is it now, Mr Ferrier? Very far?

John Ferrier: (a quietly spoken American) Oh, quite a ways, I guess.

Lucy: You can put me down now, if you like. I can walk.

John Ferrier: I don't mind carryin' you.

Lucy: (pause) Where's mother, and the others? Will we see them soon?

John Ferrier: (with certain emphasis) Yeah - I guess we will.

Lucy: Oh, good! We've such a lot to tell them, haven't we!

John Ferrier: Guess so.

Lucy: (pause) I'm thirsty. Is there any water left?

John Ferrier: (a deep breath) I'm afraid not, honey.

Lucy: What about food?

John Ferrier: That's all gone too.

LUCK: Will mother bring some when she comes?

John Ferrier: She... she won't be coming.

Lucy: (faltering) Why... why not?

John Ferrier: (kindly) She's dead, honey.

Lucy: What! Mummy's a deader?

John Ferrier: 'Fraid so; and your daddy too and your brother Bob, and Mr Bender and Indian Pete, and Johnny Hones - they're all gone. We're the only ones left.

Lucy: Are we going to die as well?

John Ferrier: You see them birds up there, circlin' over us? Well, they're buzzards, an' they sure think we're goin' to die.

Lucy: Well, they're wrong, 'cos there's lots of people coming, and I'm sure they'll help us!

John Ferrier: (laughing hollowly) Yeah...

Lucy: No, really! Look behind you!

John Ferrier: (sighs) Oh, all ri... Good God Almighty! You're right, little Lucy - but who are they!

(Return to Jefferson Hope's narrative)

There were thousands of them - a long line of covered wagons with herds of cattle, sheep, horses and goats, moving slowly and purposefully across the Utah desert. They drew near, and a group of out-riders, hard-faced, grave men armed with rifles, saw them. One, the leader, called to them.

(Return to desert scene)

Brigham Young: (huge and sonorous) Who are ye? Answer, in the name of the Lord!

John Ferrier: I'm John Ferrier; and this little girl is Lucy, my... daughter.

Brigham Young: How come ye to be wandering in the desert?

John Ferrier: We were trying to make it through to Oregon, twenty of us. We're all that's left.

Brigham Young: It is the will of God! **(The other outriders echo him in a mutter)**

John Ferrier: Who are you?

Brigham Young: We are the persecuted children of the Lord - the chosen of the Angel Moroni!

John Ferrier: He seems to have chosen a fair lot of you.

Brigham Young: Do not laugh at what is sacred! Ten thousand of us have departed from the State of Illinois to seek a refuge in the desert from the violent, godless people of the world. We are the Mormons!

(The others echo him again) We are the Mormons!

John Ferrier: Where are you going?

Brigham Young: The Lord will show us. But if we take you with us it must be as true believers in our creed - as fellow Mormons - otherwise we leave you here to die. Do you accept?

John Ferrier: (laughs) Ain't got much choice. All right then, why not.

Brigham Young: Remember - you are now of our religion. I, Brigham Young have said it; and I speak with the voice of the prophet Joseph Smith, who is the voice of God! (To the others) Let us go, my brothers! On, on - to Zion!

ALL: To Zion! To Zion! (fade out)

(Return to Hope's narrative)

Jeff Hope: So John and Lucy Ferrier joined the Mormons, or Latter Day Saints as they were also called, and helped to found their temple at Salt Lake City. In return John was given land which he worked; and so well that within a dozen years there was not a richer man among them. And as for Lucy, she grew more beautiful every day, until, when she was 18 years of age, there was no more lovely woman in the State. The Flower of Utah she was called. And then, when it seemed that all happiness could and should be theirs, came tragedy instead.

PART FOUR

CAST:

Mr Sherlock Holmes	Brigham Young
Dr John Watson	John Ferrier
Inspector Lestrade	Lucy Ferrier: - now aged about 18
Inspector Gregson	
Jefferson Hope	

Dr Watson: (**Narration**) Jefferson Hope, the killer of Enoch Drebber and Joseph Stangerson, had been caught. Now he was telling us his story; how it started thirty years ago with a man named John Ferrier and his little girl, Lucy, who were found in the desert by the Mormons and taken in by them; how Ferrier grew to be a rich man and Lucy the loveliest woman in the State of Utah.

(**Scene:** the interrogation room of Scotland Yard)
Jeff Hope: She grew up in Salt Lake City. Then, when she had turned 18, two things happened to her: one good - and the other, very bad.
The good thing was that we met, she and I, and fell in love. I was a hunter then, and prospector for gold, was not a Mormon and didn't live in Salt Lake City. I needed money for my bride - for we were going to marry - I even had the ring - so I went away to find it in the hills. Two months was all I needed.

Then came the second thing - the bad one. Mormons, as you know, have several wives, and John Ferrier, though a Mormon too, had never married. This made him suspect in the leaders' eyes; which was a bad thing to be, for the Mormon Church was run by four men - the Holy Four - and to disagree with or to disobey them was very dangerous indeed.

Three weeks after I had left, John Ferrier had a visitor - Brigham Young himself, the leader of the Mormons. But it was not a friendly visit...

(**Scene:** Ferrier's farm near Salt Lake City)
Brigham Young: (thunderously) Is it true, then, that your daughter, Brother Ferrier, is engaged to some Gentile, one not a Mormon? I do not believe it! What is our 13th Rule? "Let every maiden of the Faith marry one of the Elect, or she commits a grievous sin". No, I do not believe it. Nonetheless, you shall be tested. Elder Drebber has a son and so has Elder Stangerson. Let her choose between them.

John Ferrier: She is young, sir. She is scarcely of an age to marry.

Brigham Young: She shall have a month to choose - no more! And remember! (his voice thunders) It were better that you died out in the desert than that you set yourself against the Holy Four!

(Exits, crashing-to the door: another door opens softly)

Lucy: Father - I heard everything. What shall we do!

John Ferrier: (with wry humour) Which do you fancy then? Young Drebber or young Stangerson?

Lucy: I'd rather die than have either! Drebber has seven wives already and is a beast in human form; and Stangerson, who has four, is only interested in your property!

John Ferrier: And young Hope?

Lucy: (voice breaks) I love him father. I will not - I could not marry anybody else.

John Ferrier: (takes a deep breath) Well, I guess that's it, then. We go.

Lucy: Go! Where?

John Ferrier: (grimly) The hell away from here! Truth is, Lucy, this ain' the first time I've considered it. I've had enough. I'm a free-born American and I won't be pushed around. And as for coming here and telling me who my daughter's got to marry - No, Sir!

Lucy: But how will we leave? What about the Holy Four?

John Ferrier: We've got a month. In that time I'll send word to young Jeff. When he comes we'll leave for Carson City in Nevada - start again. And Stangerson and Drebber - and the whole damn lot of 'em - are welcome to whatever I leave behind!

(Return to Jefferson Hope in Scotland Yard)

Jeff Hope: Brave words, gentlemen, from a brave and honourable man. I came back as soon as I got word; but I came too late. There was his grave underneath a tree, and the sign: 'John Ferrier, died 4th August, 1860. The Holy Four had gotten him. (Pause) And Lucy? (pause) I met a man who told me. She was married but two days before - to young Drebber. Stangerson had killed her father - he therefore had first claim; but Drebber was the richer, so he got her. But not for long. Within a month she too, was dead, pining away and dying of a broken heart.

(His voice roughens) And so I swore - I swore an oath - that I would not rest until John Ferrier and his daughter were avenged. Enoch Drebber and Joseph Stangerson would die, and I was going to kill them, no matter how long it might take.

It took, in fact, twenty years. They knew that I was after them and they started running. First to Cleveland, in Ohio, where they had me thrown in jail. Then to Europe; to St Petersburg in Russia; to Paris, France; to Copenhagen, Denmark - always running. Finally London - where I caught up with them - at last! (pause) I think you know the rest.

Holmes: Not entirely. I've one or two questions for you.

Jeff Hope: Go ahead.

Holmes: The poisoned pills. What were they about?

Jeff Hope: I'm a religious man, sir, - even if I ain't a Mormon. Those men were dogs and both deserved to die. But I don't kill even dogs in cold blood; there has to be a chance. So I had the pills made up, one harmless and one lethal: he had first choice and let Almighty God decide. I picked up Drebber and took him to an empty house I knew in Brixton. There he had his choice - and died - with Lucy Ferrier's wedding-ring before his eyes and my curse in his ears.

Holmes: And Stangerson? How did you know where he was staying?

Jeff Hope: I heard them talking earlier. I used a ladder to climb into Stangerson's room, where I gave him the same choice I gave Drebber. He made a fight of it instead, so I stabbed him through the heart.

Insp. Lestrade: What does 'Rache' mean? Why did you write it on the wall?

Jeff Hope: (laughing) I wasn't going to swing for killing a couple of dogs! I did it to confuse you, to make you think it was Anarchists or something.

Insp. Gregson: And the blood you wrote it with? Where did that come from?

Jeff Hope: From me.

Insp. Gregson: Oh?

Jeff Hope: You're a Doctor, ain't you?

Dr Watson: (startled) Who, me? Yes - I'm a doctor.

Jeff Hope: Put your hand here, against my chest. There - do you feel it?

Dr Watson: Why - yes! Good Lord - you've got an... an aortic aneurism.

Jeff Hope: Right first time. The old heart's in real bad shape. Sometimes the pressure is so high it makes my nose bleed - like it did the night I exterminated Drebber. That's where the blood came from.

Insp. Lestrade: Is it dangerous, Doctor?

Dr Watson: It certainly is! His heart could burst at any moment!

Insp. Gregson: We'd better get him into bed, then. We don't want him to die before he hangs!

Jeff Hope: (laughs) In that case I'll go. But afterwards, perhaps you, Mr Holmes, would be good enough to tell these gentlemen from Scotland Yard just how you found me?

Holmes: If they ask me.

Jeff Hope: Oh, they'll ask you! They've been scratching their thick heads since yesterday, wondering how you did it. My compliments, sir.

Holmes: A pleasure, Mr Hope, and goodbye. (Exit Hope: door closes) Coughing from Lestrade and Gregson)

Holmes: (after a pointed pause) Well, Watson - shall we go?

Insp. Lestrade: (quickly) Just a minute, Mr Holmes. I do think you owe us an explanation...

Holmes: (wrathfully) A what!

Insp. Lestrade: (hastily) I mean, if you'd be kind enough to explain... Inspector Gregson?

Insp. Gregson: (coughs) Well, er, yes... we would appreciate a little information if you don't mind.

Holmes: (pause) Very well. It was by observation and deduction. From the tracks in the road outside the house in Brixton I observed that a cab had drawn up. Footprints showed that two men had entered. One belonged to the man lying dead: the other, therefore, was the man who poisoned him. Who was he? While the two men were inside, the cab-horse had wandered down the street - which it would not have done had the cabby still been there. Answer: the second man must be the cab-driver.

Insp. Lestrade: How did you know the murdered man was poisoned?

Holmes: I smelt it on his lips when I examined him. The question then motive: - why? The answer was not the German writing on the wall, for it was not written in the German way and too obviously a blind. It was the ring. The motive was a woman - a wife - either Drebber's or the cab-driver's.

Insp. Gregson: How did you discover his name?

Holmes: She must have been connected with their mutual past. Drebber's card showed that he had lived in Cleveland, Ohio, so I telegraphed the head of the Police there, asking for details of any threats against his life. There had been - by an old rival in love named Jefferson Hope. Case complete.

Insp. Lestrade: How did you find him?

Holmes: My Baker Street Irregulars found him.

Insp. Gregson: (with frightful condescension) Hmmm, well, quite neatly done, I dare say. We'd have found him for ourselves, of course, in time; but not bad, all the same. Eh, Lestrade?

Insp. Lestrade: (pompously) You've been a very lucky man, Mr Holmes. A very... lucky man... (fade out)

Dr Watson: (Narration) So ended my first case with Sherlock Holmes. And yet, not quite. Two days later Jefferson Hope died in his cell; and on the same day, in the London Daily Echo, appeared an article...

(**Scene:** Holmes' rooms at 221b Baker Street)

Dr Watson: (in a voice of outrage, rustling the newspaper) Look at this Holmes: "... it is an open secret that the credit for the smart capture of Jefferson Hope belongs entirely to those two well-known Scotland Yard officials Inspectors Lestrade and Gregson."!

Holmes: Well?

Dr Watson: It's not true! It's a damned disgrace! Someone ought to show them up! Make them pay for their lies and inefficiency!

Holmes: My dear Watson, I don't care what papers write or people think. The case was solved by me - that's all that really matters. That and perhaps one other thing.

Dr Watson: What?

Holmes: That the earth will not cease to revolve about the sun; that spring will come, the flowers return, crime continue here in London and that Gregson and Lestrade will be back for my assistance. (His voice hardens) And I'll make them pay - don't worry about that! (He laughs. Dr Watson joins him in laughter and the scene fades).

My Case Notes and Glossary

The Illustrious Client

by Sir Arthur Conan Doyle
Dramatised by Michael Mandeville

Cast
Sherlock Holmes
Sir James Damery (an English gentleman)
Dr James Watson
Kitty Winter (a young Cockney woman)
Violet de Merville (a young gentlewoman)
Baron Adelbart Gruner (an Austrian nobleman)

(**Scene:** Holmes' Rooms at 221b, Baker Street, London. Year: 1902.)

Holmes: What's the time, Watson?
Dr Watson: Just coming up to half past four. Are you expecting someone?
Holmes: Yes... Sir James Damery,
Dr Watson: (interested) Oh, really?
Holmes: Do you know him?
Dr Watson: I know *of* him. A worthy man: something of a diplomat who negotiates delicate matters in which people in Society are concerned - in other words, scandal. Hardly your business, I would have thought.
Holmes: Scandal has been known to end in serious crime. Perhaps this is why Sir James wishes to see me. (the sound of a distant doorbell) Ah - that sounds like him now. Do you mind staying, Watson?
Dr Watson: Not at all, my dear fellow. Be delighted (fade out)
Holmes: ... to prevent a marriage did you say, Sir James? (laughs) Come, come - I deal in crime. Marriage is hardly that!
Damery: Sometimes it can lead to it, Mr Holmes.
Holmes: That depends. Who is the woman Involved?
Damery: She is Violet de Merville, only child of General de Merville.
Dr Watson: I think I've heard of her. Very rich, very beautiful, is she not? Her husband-to-be is a lucky man.
Damery: (drily) Quite so.
Holmes: Who is he, Sir James?
Damery: He is Baron Adalbert Gruner.
Holmes: The Austrian? From Budapest?
Damery: The same.

Holmes: (thoughtfully) I see. That rather changes matters then, doesn't it.

Dr Watson: Do you know him Holmes?

Holmes: Indeed I do. He too, is very rich, very good-looking.

Dr Watson: (chuckles) What is wrong with that?

Holmes: He has been married twice before, each time to a wealthy woman who died under violent and peculiar circumstances. Nothing was ever proved, but apart from these activities the dear Baron is well known in the Continental underworld as a clever and ruthless criminal.

Dr Watson: Good Lord!

Damery: I see you have most of the facts, Mr Holmes. Perhaps you can understand why I fear for Miss de Merville's safety.

Dr Watson: But surely, Sir James, if the Baron's character is as bad as that, can she not be told of it? Would that not be enough to dissuade her from marriage?

Damery: Unfortunately not. She is utterly and completely in love with him.

Holmes: In love, eh. Does she know about his first two wives?

Damery: Certainly. The Baron has told her everything but always in such a way as to make himself the innocent party. She accepts his version and will listen to no other.

Holmes: What do you want me to do?

Damery: I have no idea. The marriage is to be stopped, that is all. How you accomplish it, I leave to you. Your fees are guaranteed to any figure you care to name.

Holmes: That is handsome of you Sir James. Very well, I shall look into the matter. I will be in touch with you.

Damery: I am indebted Mr Holmes. Gentlemen, I bid you good day ... (fade out)

Holmes: Well, Watson - a pretty problem. Where do we go from here?

Dr Watson: Couldn't you go and see the girl yourself and try and dissuade her?

Holmes: I do not doubt that her father, her mother, her friends and relatives, have all tried, and that I would be as unsuccessful as they. No, it will have to be done in another way. But first, let us go for the man himself: Baron Gruner is someone I have always wanted to meet. You have his record there Watson; where does he live?

Dr Watson: At Vernon Lodge, near Kingston. Would you like me to come with you?

Holmes: Not this time, my dear fellow. It would be better if I went alone. (fade out)

(**Scene:** Baron Gruner's drawing room)

Baron Gruner: (a suave man of 40) Ah, my dear Mr Holmes, I have been expecting you. Pray sit down. I believe you have been engaged by someone to put a stop to my forthcoming marriage to Miss de Merville - am I correct?

Holmes: Quite correct, Baron Gruner.

Baron Gruner: May I enquire what you propose?

Holmes: Of course. We both know about each other, so there is no need for subterfuge. No one wants to investigate your past. It is over and you are now a respectable citizen. But if you persist in this marriage you will raise up a swarm of powerful enemies who will never leave you alone until they have made England too hot to hold you. I ask you - is it worth it? Surely it would be wiser to leave the lady alone. It would not be pleasant if the facts of your past were brought to her notice.

Baron Gruner: (chuckling) Forgive my amusement, Mr Holmes, but it is rather funny to see you trying to play a hand with no cards in it. You will never find anything against me and even if you did I have already warned Miss de Merville of what you intend, and she is ready for you. She will listen, but she will take no notice.

Holmes: So you think.

Baron Gruner: So I know. Have you heard of 'hypnotic suggestion'? I see you have. Believe me, Miss de Merville is an excellent subject.

Holmes: In that case there is no more to discuss.

Baron Gruner: Indeed there is not. I would be grateful therefore, if you would forget the whole matter. Leave me to go my way, and I will leave you to go yours.

Holmes: I cannot promise that.

Baron Gruner: As you like. But before you go ... do you remember the case of the French detective, Monsieur le Brun?

Holmes: Yes. He was attacked and crippled for life by an unknown gang in Paris last year.

Baron Gruner: Exactly. And it is no coincidence that he had recently been inquiring into some affairs of mine. Remember, Mr Holmes, I am a man who says rather less than he means ... (fade out)

(**Scene:** Holmes' rooms)

Holmes: He was like a cat, Watson, a great, purring cat. He sits there in his beautiful drawing-room, surrounded by his collection of Chinese porcelain - did I tell you he was an expert on porcelain? - and he dared me to try and get the better of him!

Dr Watson: What will you do now?

Holmes: I think ... I shall set a thief to catch a thief; I have my contacts in the underworld, as you know, and ... (there is a knock at the door)

Dr Watson: Who is that?

Holmes: (opening the door to Kitty Winter, a Cockney girl) Good evening.

Kitty: Hullo, Are you Mr Sherlock Holmes?

Holmes: I am.

Kitty: I heard ... you was lookin' for some information about ... Adelbert Gruner.

Holmes: Did you. Won't you come in? Sit down. This is Dr Watson.

Kitty: How d'ye do, sir,

Dr Watson: How do you do.

Holmes: Well now, what can you tell me about Mr Gruner?

Kitty: (venomously) He's a devil, that's what he is! You needn't ask me about my past, Mr Holmes: that doesn't matter. But what I am, Adelbert Gruner made me - and I want revenge!

Holmes: Do you know what all this is about?

Kitty: Oh yes. He's after some other woman. Only this time he wants to marry her. But that should be easy enough to stop. Just tell her about him.

Holmes: That's already been tried. She will not listen.

Kitty: Give her proof.

Holmes: What proof?

Kitty: Ain't I proof enough if I stood before her and told her how he used me ...

Holmes: But would you do this?

Kitty: Would I! Just give me the chance!

Holmes: Hmmm ...

Dr Watson: It might work, Holmes.

Holmes: (undecided) Possibly. But he has told her all about himself and she has forgiven him everything.

Kitty: I'll bet he never told her about his book!

Holmes: Book? What book?

Kitty: A brown leather book, what he keeps somewhere in his study. I've seen it. It's a record of all his women, their names, their photographs, their details - the sort of book no man should ever have. She'll be in it, and all the other women he's ever ruined. I'm in it, too.

Holmes: I'm sorry about that, Kitty. But we'll see if we can't stop him this time. I shall take you to the lady in question first thing tomorrow morning ... (fade out)

(**Scene:** Miss de Merville's salon)

Holmes: Good morning, Miss de Merville. My name is Sherlock Holmes.

Miss de Merville: (cold, distant) Your name is known to me, Mr Holmes. You have called, as I understand, to blacken the character of my fiancé Baron Gruner. It is only at my father's request that I see you at all, and I warn you in advance that nothing you say will influence me in the least.

Holmes: Perhaps not, Miss de Merville. But if I could refer you to newspaper reports, reputable witnesses ...

Miss de Merville: It is useless. I am aware that Adelbert has had a stormy life, and has incurred bitter hatred and unjust criticism. But if his noble nature has ever, for an instant fallen, I regard myself as having been sent specially to raise it to its true and lofty level. On one point however, I am not entirely clear: who . . . is this young lady?

Kitty: (springing forward, furiously) I'll tell you who I am! I'm your fiancé's last mis-

tress! I'm one of a hundred he has tempted and used and ruined, and thrown onto the rubbish heap - as he will you, too! - Only your rubbish heap will more likely be a grave. I tell you, you stupid woman, that if you marry him he'll be the death of you - a broken heart or a broken neck, he'll kill you one way or the other. And it's not out of love for you I'm telling you this! I don't care if you live or die. It's out of hate for him, revenge for what he did to me! No - you needn't look at me like that, my fine lady. One day you'll be as low as I am!

Miss de Merville: I should prefer not to discuss such matters. I know my fiancé has allowed himself to become entangled with designing women, and that he repents these three occasions . . .

Kitty: Three occasions! Three! You fool! You stupid little fool!

Miss de Merville: Mr Holmes, I beg you will bring this interview to an end immediately!

Holmes: Come along, Kitty. Time to go home.

Kitty: (beside herself) She's mad ! He's hypnotised her! Can't you see it? She's let herself be hypnotised. (fade out)

(**Scene:** Holmes' rooms)

Dr Watson: Well, Holmes, any luck this time?

Holmes: No, Watson, but we have not finished yet.

Dr Watson: What is your next step?

Holmes: How well do you know Dr Hill Barton?

Dr Watson: (bewildered) I don't know him at all!

Holmes: Good. Neither does Baron Gruner. Dr Hill Barton, you see, is you.

Dr Watson: Me!

Holmes: Yes. Now pay attention! There is something I want you to do, and it's not going to be easy ... (fade out)

(**Scene:** Baron Gruner's drawing-room)

Baron Gruner: Dr Hill Barton, good evening. I am Baron Gruner. I received your note this morning. You say you are a collector of porcelain and that you have a set of six saucers from the Ming Dynasty you wish to sell. Have you brought a specimen with you?

Dr Watson: Of course ... (rustle of paper) Here.

Baron Gruner: Thank you. Hmmm - very fine indeed. The finest! I know of only one such set in all England. Would it be indiscreet, Dr Hill Barton, to ask you where you obtained this?

Dr Watson: (drily) Yes, Baron, it would.

Baron Gruner: I see. But why do you come to me?

Dr Watson: I understood you were a connoisseur.

Baron Gruner: Correct. You must have read my book.

Dr Watson: No, in fact ...

Baron Gruner: (sharply) Why not?

Dr Watson: No time. I'm a busy man, a doctor in practice ...

Baron Gruner: That is no answer. If a man has a hobby he follows it up. You said you were a connoisseur - then let me ask you some questions.

Dr Watson: Whatever you like.

Baron Gruner: What do you know of the Emporer Shumu, and what is his connection with the Shoso-in near Tsra? What do you know of the Northern Wei Dynasty?

Dr Watson: I ...

Baron Gruner: Nothing, Dr Hill Barton! I guess from your face! You are a fraud! Probably a spy of Sherlock Holmes. Wait! What is that? Someone is in my study! (rushes across the room, flings open the door) You – stop! My God – it's Kitty Winter! What ...

Kitty: (quietly) Hullo, Adalbert.

Baron Gruner: (roughly) What are you doing here?

 Kitty: I came to get this.

Baron Gruner: My book! Give it to me at once.

Kitty: With pleasure. Take that - you swine!

 Baron Gruner: Ah! (he screams) Ah, my eyes! My eyes!
(there is a general hubbub: the voice of Holmes calls Kitty urgently; a scuffle, a cry, the sound of breaking glass, a falling body)

Baron Gruner: (still screaming) Vitriol! She's thrown vitriol into my eyes! Hill Barton - are you there? You're a doctor - do something!

Dr Watson: Yes, I'm here, I'm here. Just lie still. Here is some water. Let me see your face. (change of tone) Oh ... My God ... (fade out)

(**Scene:** Holmes' rooms)

 Dr Watson: He's blind, Holmes, totally. He'll never see again.

Holmes: (much shaken) A terrible business ... terrible ...

Dr Watson: Did you know she was carrying vitriol - what she was going to do?

Holmes: I had no idea. I was after the book. She was going to show me where it was, that's all.

Dr Watson: What an end. I feel almost sorry for the man.

Holmes: (grimly) You needn't. Miss de Merville has now seen the book.

Dr Watson: (sarcastic) Has she. I hope she is finally convinced.

Holmes: I think so. The Baron's opinion of her was even lower than yours - and her name had already been crossed through. Without doubt she was to be wife number three, who unfortunately died.

My Case Notes and Glossary

Sherlock Holmes and the Naval Treaty

by Sir Arthur Conan Doyle
Dramatised by Michael Mandeville

Cast
Sherlock Holmes
Dr James Watson
Joseph Harrison
Percy Phelps
Annie Harrison
Lord Holdhurst

(**Scene:** Holmes' rooms at 221b Baker Street, London. Year: 1890)
Dr Watson: I say, Holmes - listen to this! (he reads)
"My Dear Watson, A dreadful thing has happened to me and I desperately need the help of you and your friend Mr Sherlock Holmes. I cannot tell you the details as the matter is of the gravest importance. The police say there is nothing they can do. My career is ruined. I have been in bed with a nervous breakdown for the past nine weeks. Please, I beg of you, please come as soon as possible. Your old schoolfellow - Percy Phelps"
Holmes: He certainly sounds upset. What career is he talking about?
Dr Watson: He holds an important position in the Foreign Office.
Holmes: May I see that letter?
Dr Watson: Certainly.
Holmes: Hmmm - interesting. I think I shall look into this. The address is Woking: we can take a train from Waterloo. Come along, Watson; after nine weeks we don't want to waste any more time, do we. (fade out)

(**Scene:** outside Phelps' house)
Dr Watson: This must be the place. (rings doorbell)
Holmes: It's very large.
Dr Watson: Someone's coming.
(The door is opened by Joseph Harrison. He is a man in his thirties, confident, a little aggressive)
Joseph Harrison: Good morning, good morning! You are Dr Watson - and you must be Mr Sherlock Holmes. We've been expecting you!
Holmes: So I see. But you are not a member of the family.
Joseph Harrison: (taken aback) Me? Oh – yes - you noticed the monogram on my locket. I'm sorry - I should have introduced myself. My name is Joseph Harrison.

Percy is engaged to my sister Annie. We are down here on a visit. She is with him now. Won't you come this way? (fade out)

(Percy Phelps is aged about 30, eager, intense)

Phelps: Watson, my dear fellow - I'm so glad you could come! And this it Sherlock Holmes - how do you do, sir! Allow me to introduce my fiancée, Miss Annie Harrison,

Holmes: How do you do. Are you the one who has been nursing Mr Phelps?

(Annie Harrison is a young woman, quiet and composed)

Annie Harrison: Oh yes, every day. A professional nurse looks after him at night.

Holmes: What a bright and cheerful room this is - right onto the garden. You must enjoy the view.

Phelps: (laughing) You'd better ask Joseph about that - it's his room!

Holmes: Oh?

Annie Harrison: Actually, Mr Holmes, it is a guest room. When Percy was taken ill he moved in here, as it's more convenient for an invalid to be on the ground floor.

Phelps: Not for very much longer, though!

Annie Harrison: And not before time. There has already been one burglary attempt since you've been here.

Holmes: Indeed! What burglary attempt?

Phelps: (dismissive) Oh, it's nothing. Some fellow tried to break in one night; but I was awake and gave the alarm. He ran away.

Holmes: I thought there was a night-nurse here?

Annie Harrison: She was off duty. Since then I have made sure someone has been with Percy all the time.

Joseph Harrison: Altogether the poor lad has had rather a bad time. But I think Mr Holmes would prefer to hear his story from the beginning: I suggest therefore, that Annie and I leave the three of you here together. We'll come back when you've finished.

Phelps: It began on the 23rd May, Hr Holmes, at six o'clock in the evening. Lord Holdhurst, the Foreign Minister, called me into his office ...

Lord Holdhurst: (grave, dignified, courteous) ... this is the original of the secret treaty between England and Italy. It defines the position of Great Britain towards the triple Alliance, and her policy should the French or Russian fleets take control of the Mediterranean. The matters dealt with are purely naval, and it has been signed by all the ministers involved. It is of great importance that nothing of it should be known. As you can imagine, the French or Russian Embassies would pay a lot to learn of it.

Phelps: Of course, sir. What do you want me to do?

Lord Holdhurst: I want it copied as soon as possible. When you have finished, lock both the original and the copy in your desk until you hand them over to me.
Phelps: Very good, sir ...
(return to narrative)

Phelps: I took the document into my office, drew the curtains and began working. It was very long and by nine o'clock I was only half-way. My intention was to work through until eleven o'clock when I was to meet Joseph at Waterloo to take the train back to Woking, but already I was getting tired. I thought a cup of coffee would wake me up and so I rang the bell for the porter. There was no answer and so I went along to his room to see what was the matter. He was fast asleep. I awakened him and was giving him my order when to my surprise the bell in his office rang. "Who is that?" I asked, for I thought everyone in the building had left. "That's from your office, sir" said the man. "My office! But ..." I rushed back. The copy of the treaty was still on my desk where I had been working on it. But the original - was gone! (pause) It was a terrible moment.
Holmes: How many doors are there to your office?
Phelps: There are two. One leads down a corridor to the porter's room. The second, which is a small, private entrance, goes from my office down a small passage directly to the street.
Holmes: Ha!
Phelps: Since I myself had used the main corridor, the thief must have entered by the second door.
Holmes: How long were you away?
Phelps: Two or three minutes, no more.
Holmes: What did you do then?
Phelps: I ran back to the porter and sent him for the police. They came and we searched high and low, but without finding a single clue. And I was not able to help them much, as, you will understand, I was quite unable to tell them exactly what had been stolen.
Holmes: Of course.
Phelps: I was desperate. I didn't know what to do. I came home to Woking early the following morning; but not until I arrived did I realise how bad was my position, and when I did I'm afraid I had a nervous breakdown. The doctor put me straight to bed and here I have stayed ever since. Yesterday was my first to be fully conscious.
Holmes: Is there anyone whom you suspect of having taken this document?
Phelps: No, no one.
Holmes: My last question: was anyone besides Lord Holdhurst aware that you had the treaty in your possession?
Phelps: On my honour, Mr Holmes, there is no one. That to me is the most puzzling

thing of all. How could the thief have known ... (fade out)

(**Scene:** a railway carriage)
Dr Watson: The most puzzling thing to me, Holmes, was the matter of that bell! Why on earth should the thief ring it at the very moment he was committing a crime?
Holmes: Mmmm. He obviously had a reason.
 Dr Watson: Obviously, but can you think of one?
Holmes: Yes, but I need more evidence.
Dr Watson: Where do you propose to find it?
Holmes: With Lord Holdhurst. I think perhaps he has the clue we are looking for - though I doubt that even he is aware of it. (fade out)

(**Scene:** the office of the Foreign Minister)
Holmes: ... and so I hope, Lord Holdhurst, you will forgive this intrusion.
Lord Holdhurst: Not at all, Mr Holmes. I am happy to help you.
Holmes: I have really only one question. When you gave the document to Mr Phelps, did you explain the grave results which would follow if the contents became known?
Lord Holdhurst: I did.
Holmes: And have there been any grave results?
Lord Holdhurst: (hesitating) No - not yet.
Holmes: If the treaty had reached, let us say, the French or Russian embassies, would you expect to have heard of it?
Lord Holdhurst: Yes, I certainly would.
Holmes: Since nearly ten weeks have passed and nothing has been heard, is it fair to assume the treaty has not reached them?
Lord Holdhurst: It is.
Holmes: Perhaps the thief is waiting for a better price?
Lord Holdhurst: If he waits any longer he will get no price at all. In a short while the treaty will be made public.
Holmes: Thank you, Lord Holdhurst; that is all I wanted to know. (fade out)

(**Scene:** a street scene)
Dr Watson: Well, Holmes, what did you think of him?
Holmes: He is a fine fellow, but he has a struggle to keep up his position. He is far from rich and has many calls. You noticed, of course, that his shoes had been re-soled?
Dr Watson: Good Heavens, Holmes - do you suspect everybody?

Holmes: Naturally. That is my job. And now, I think, we will return to Woking, to see what progress in health young Phelps has made. (fade out)

(**Scene**: rural background, birdsong etc)
Dr Watson: Here we are. And there is Annie Harrison, picking flowers in the garden.
Holmes: Excellent, Just the person I wanted to see. (raises his voice) Good afternoon, Miss Harrison. I trust I find you well?
Annie Harrison: Well enough, Mr Holmes, thank you.
Holmes: And your fiancé? In good spirits? (a little anxiously) Where is he?
Annie Harrison: In his room, Mr Holmes, as always. I have followed your instructions exactly.
Holmes: Good.
Annie Harrison: And I think it well I did so.
Holmes: Aha - Another visitor
Annie Harrison: Correct - though how did you know?
Holmes: Never mind. What happened?
Annie Harrison: Nothing. The night nurse said she heard a noise outside, but when she went to investigate the burglar ran off into the darkness.
Holmes: Good. Now listen carefully: there is something else I want you to do ... (fade out)

(**Scene:** Interior of the house)
Holmes: ... and so I think it better, Mr Phelps, if the three of us were to return to London this evening to complete our enquiries.
Phelps: Wonderful! (anxiously) But what about Annie? Will you be all right here?
Annie Harrison: Of course I will. Joseph will be in the house, as well as your parents.
Phelps: Very well, then. That is settled. Will you help me pack my bag? Joseph will run us to the station.

(**Scene:** a railway station, a train, receding)
Phelps: (bewildered) But why are we getting off here, Mr Holmes? This is only the next station! Where are you going now?
Holmes: Back to your house, Mr Phelps.
Phelps: What?
Dr Watson: You must trust my friend, Percy. He knows what he's doing.
Phelps: (doubtfully) Oh, very well, then. But it's getting dark already.
Holmes: The darker the better. Come along now, we've no time to lose. (fade out)

(**Scene:** night owls hooting, and the sound of stealthy movement among bushes)
Phelps: (whispering) Look - there is Annie, sitting in my room, reading. I can see her

clearly.

Holmes: (whispering) Right ... In a moment she will get up, turn out the light and lock the door behind her.

Phelps: How do you know?

Holmes: Because I told her to.

Phelps: What?

Holmes: Shhh! There she goes. Good girl. Now we must wait. (fade out)

Phelps: (whispering) Brrr, it's getting cold. How much longer do you ...

Holmes: Shhh! Here he comes!

Phelps: Who?

Holmes: Your burglar.

Phelps: Good Heavens!

Dr Watson: He's going to the window. Look! He's opening it! (sound of creaking)

Holmes: Now he's gone inside. Have you your torch, Watson?

Dr Watson: Yes.

Holmes: Then we will follow him. No noise now.

(The sound of quiet footsteps! then Holmes's shout) Got you! (A cry, the sound of struggle, blows, grunts and exclamations of pain)

Phelps: (a shout of delight) The treaty! The naval treaty! Here it is, on the floor! I've found it!

Holmes: (breathless) The torch, man! Pick up the torch! Let's see who we have caught here ...

Phelps: Wait ... wait ... Here it is. Why! (a voice of horror) It's Joseph! (fade out)

(**Scene:** Holmes's rooms in Baker Street)

Holmes: The essence of criminal investigation, Watson, is logic. When a man rings a bell, it is to call someone. This, Joseph Harrison, arriving early at the Foreign Office in search of Percy Phelps and finding no one there, logically did. At the same instant that he rang, however, he saw a document lying on the desk, recognised its value, snatched it up and was gone. He took an earlier train home, and, as soon as he could, he hid it. Where? Logically, in his room. Where else could he, a visitor to London, hide it?

Dr Watson: You mean his presence at the Foreign Office was an accident?

Holmes: Of course. If no one but Lord Holdhurst knew Phelps had the treaty, then it had to be. But then the unexpected happened: Phelps arrived home later, took ill and Joseph was bundled out of his room for nine whole weeks. Logically he tried to get the treaty back, of course, by simple burglary, but each time he failed.

Dr Watson: And poor Percy was lying with the treaty not two feet from his head!

Holmes: This also had to be, or logically the treaty would have reappeared - as Lord Holdhurst said.

Dr Watson: I follow your reasoning, Holmes; yet in one particular, logic is absent. What could possess a man to rob not only his friend and host, but also discredit his own future brother-in-law?

Holmes: (sighing) Ah, there you have it. For men like Joseph Harrison, such infamous behaviour is logical. That is why they are criminals! And why, for men like me, there is always work to do. It is an ill wind, my dear Watson, that blows nobody any good.

My Case Notes and Glossary

The Sussex Vampire

by Sir Arthur Conan Doyle
Dramatised by Michael Mandeville

Cast
Sherlock Holmes
Robert Ferguson (a man of fifty)
Dr James Watson
Marie Ferguson (his wife: a South American of 35)
Jacky Ferguson (his son, aged 15)

(**Scene:** Holmes' rooms at 221b Baker Street, London)
Dr Watson: Tell me, Holmes - what do you know about 'vampires'?
Holmes: It's a large species of bat from South America - obtains its food by sucking the blood of living creatures. It ...
Dr Watson: I meant ... human vampires.
Holmes: (with asperity) Then you had better refer to Hans Andersen and the Brothers Grimm. We are a Detective Agency, Watson - not collectors of fairy-tales.
Dr Watson: (crushed) Oh ...
Holmes: Why do you ask?
Dr Watson: I have just received a letter from an old friend, Bob Ferguson who tells me that a friend of his has on two occasions caught his wife sucking the blood from the neck of their little baby.
Holmes: You seem to have some peculiar friends, Watson ...
Dr Watson: No need for sarcasm. Holmes. Bob Ferguson is one of the finest men I know.
Holmes: Perhaps ... you had better read me his letter.
Dr Watson: Very well. He says: "My friend married a Peruvian lady and brought her back to England. He was married before and already had a son, a sweet-natured boy of fifteen. A few weeks after they arrived, his new wife suddenly, brutally and for no reason assaulted her step-son on two separate occasions, once with her hands and once with a stick. But her behaviour towards her own child was even worse. A month ago the baby's nurse heard it crying: she went to it and found the mother bent over the cradle, apparently biting the baby's neck and causing it to bleed. The lady implored the nurse not to tell the father, and gave her five pounds to buy her silence. The nurse kept quiet; but it was obvious that the mother was continually watching the baby and wanted to get at it again, and the nurse became so worried that in the end she went to the master and told him everything. At first he did not believe her; but then, even as they were speaking, they heard a cry, and rushing

upstairs found the mother again bending over the cradle. There was blood on the baby's neck; and when the husband turned his wife's face to the light, there was also blood upon her mouth. She gave no explanation but ran straight to her room, locked herself in and refused to talk to anyone. All this was yesterday. The baby has been returned to the care of the nurse. My poor friend is almost dead from worry. I wonder if you could ask Mr Sherlock Holmes to help him. Your old chum - Bob Ferguson.

Holmes: What an extraordinary story! Where does all this take place?

Dr Watson: At Lamberley, in Sussex.

Holmes: Not too far. Well, you had better send Mr Ferguson a telegram: "Will investigate your case with pleasure".

Dr Watson: Your case?

Holmes: We do not want him to think this Agency is a home for the weak minded. Of course it is his case. I suggest you make the appointment for ten o'clock tomorrow morning. (fade out)

Holmes: Your letter was very clear, Mr Ferguson. However before we start you will forgive me if I ask you bluntly: do you believe your wife to be entirely sane?

Ferguson: (haggard, earnest) Absolutely and completely sane, Mr Holmes. That is what I cannot understand - what is driving me mad! And not only is she sane, but I know she loves me with her whole heart!

Holmes: And the baby?

Ferguson: Is her own child! She adores it!

Holmes: But has no affection for the son of your first marriage, it appears. What is his name?

Ferguson: Jacky. No, that I cannot understand either. He is so young, and a dear lad with a loving heart. And he is a cripple too: he had a fall when he was little and cannot walk properly. Yet she beat him, savagely, twice.

Holmes: Why? Did he give any reason?

Ferguson: No. He said there was none.

Holmes: Are they good friends at other times?

Ferguson: No. There is no love between them.

Holmes: Yet you say he affectionate.

Ferguson: To me he is. My life is his life. In all the world one could not have a more devoted son.

Holmes: Your wife, I believe, is from Peru.

Ferguson: Yes, an old Peruvian family. She is a real Latin, passionate, fiery...

Holmes: And jealous?

Ferguson: (hesitating) Yes ... very. She kept saying she hated him. Again and again she said so.

Holmes: And Jacky, being affectionate, was devoted no doubt, to the memory of his

mother?

Ferguson: Yes.

Holmes: Well, Mr Ferguson, all this has been most interesting. Yet I think my inquiries can best be continued at your home in Sussex. A train leaves from Victoria in an hour.

Ferguson: You will come too, Watson, will you not?

Holmes: Of course he will! I should be lost without my Watson. Come - Let us be on our way ...(fade out)

(**Scene:** Ferguson's house at Lamberley)

Ferguson: Here we are. Mind the step. This is the main hall-way and here is the drawing room. Now, gentlemen, if you will excuse me, I must know what is happening to my wife and children...

Dr Watson and Holmes: Certainly! Of course.

Ferguson: Thank you. (exits)

Holmes: This is an interesting place, Watson. Very old, I should say - four or five hundred years at least. Look at those oaken beams; and the fireplace is enormous.

Dr Watson: What interest me ... are those weapons up there on the wall: knives, bows, arrows. But they are too small to be English - where do you suppose they come from?

Holmes: Peru, I should say: souvenirs brought over by the new Mrs Ferguson.

Dr Watson: And that, over there?

Holmes: It is a blow-pipe, (reflective) Interesting ... Sometimes, Watson, you are more perceptive than you know.

Dr Watson: Glad to hear you say so. Hullo - what have we here? (sound of a dog whining) It's a cocker spaniel. Come here, boy.

Holmes: (curiously) What's the matter with him? His back legs ...

Dr Watson: Yes - they seem to be paralysed. What a shame.

Holmes: (to himself) Good ... Lord!

 (Enter Ferguson, distressed)

Ferguson: I'm sorry to have kept you waiting Watson, old man, I wonder if you'd mind ... talking to my wife. She's still locked in her room and I fear she may be ailing.

Dr Watson: Certainly! I'll go at once. (hurries out)

Holmes: By the way, Mr Ferguson - your dog. How long has it been sick like this?

Ferguson: (recovering his thoughts) The dog? Oh ... a month or so.

Holmes: What's wrong with it?

Ferguson: I don't know. The vet said it might be spinal meningitis.

Holmes: It came on suddenly, did it not?

Ferguson: Yes - in a single night. How did you know?

Holmes: I was expecting it.

Ferguson: What!

(An interruption - Jacky Ferguson enters, excited)

Jacky Ferguson: Daddy, Daddy! You're back! How lovely to see you!

Ferguson: Hullo, Jacky. How have you been?

Jacky Ferguson: Oh, I've missed you so much. You shouldn't have gone away without telling me.

Ferguson: There now, don't fret about it.

Jacky Ferguson: Who is this?

Ferguson: This is Mr Holmes.

Jacky Ferguson: Is he a friend of yours?

Ferguson: Er.. yes, he is.

Jacky Ferguson: (a little hostile) Oh. How do you do.

Holmes: How do you do, Jacky. And how is your baby brother?

Jacky Ferguson: I don't know.

Ferguson: Well, go and ask nurse to bring him, will you?

Jacky Ferguson: (almost sullen) Do you want to see him now?

Ferguson: Yes, Jacky, right away. Hurry along, won't you. (fade out)

(**Scene:** outside Mrs Ferguson's bedroom - a discreet knocking)

Marie: (speaks from the other side of the door with a strong Spanish accent) Who is there?

Dr Watson: My name is Watson, madame. I am a doctor.

Marie: Wait ... (the door is unlocked, opened) Oh! Please come in.

Dr Watson: Mrs Ferguson - you really don't look well. Sit down, here in this chair.

Marie: I do not feel well. Where is my husband?

Dr Watson: He is downstairs. He wishes to see you.

Marie: (with beginning hysteria) I will not see him! I will not see him. Oh ... (sobbing) He is a devil! A devil! What shall I do?

Dr Watson: Can I help in any way?

Marie: No; no one can help. It is finished. There is nothing I can do. (her sobs renew)

Dr Watson: Madame, your husband loves you dearly, and wants nothing but your happiness.

Marie: Then why do he say those terrible things to me? Why do he take my baby away? I love him! I sacrifice myself before I break his heart. That is how I love him!

Dr Watson: Perhaps he cannot understand.

Marie: Yes, but he should trust me!

Dr Watson: Will you not see him? '

Marie: No, no. Go now. Tell him one things that I want my child, that I must have my child ... my child ... (she weeps; fade out)

Holmes: (murmuring) So this is the child, is it. My compliments, Mr Ferguson - a

really beautiful baby.

Ferguson: Yes - he is very strong. He'll be a big man.

Holmes: And there is the mark, on his neck ...

Ferguson: (heavily) Yes ...

Jacky Ferguson: (from across the room) Daddy - here is someone else !

Ferguson: Oh, hullo, Watson. Jacky, take the baby for a moment, will you? (to Watson) How is she?

Dr Watson: In health not good. Neither does she want to see you.

Ferguson: I feared as much. What do you advise?

Dr Watson: I honestly don't know. I've never met anything like it. Perhaps Holmes ... (pauses, then raises his voice) Holmes?

Ferguson: (whispering) What's he staring at?

Dr Watson: (whispering) I don't know. Something in the window, (raises his voice again) Holmes?

Holmes: (coming to) Oh - yes?

Dr Watson: Er, Ferguson wanted to know ... what you thought about the case.

Holmes: The case? What case? The case is finished.

Dr Watson and Ferguson together: What!

Holmes: Now I should like to see Mrs Ferguson. Will you fetch her, Watson?

Dr Watson: She will not come down

Holmes: She will. Just give her this note (he scribbles) There ...

Dr Watson: Very well, (exits)

Holmes: And now you, Jacky. Give your father the baby and go and play in the garden.

Jacky Ferguson: (petulant) Oh - why?

Holmes: Because I tell you.

Ferguson: Do as he says, Jacky.

Jacky Ferguson: Oh ... (exits)

Ferguson: Mr Holmes, do you really believe you have got to the bottom of this dreadful matter?

Holmes: If your wife appears in answer to my note, then I have. And here she is!

Ferguson: (gasps) My dear one!

Marie: Roberto ! No - do not come near. Has this gentleman - has he told you the truth?

Ferguson: No, not yet.

Marie: Then he must!

Holmes: He will. But first, Mr Ferguson, return the baby to your wife.

Ferguson: Of course. There.

Marie: (crooning) My baby...

Holmes: Your wife is a loving and ill-used woman, but before I prove it to you, I fear

I must hurt you deeply in another direction.

Ferguson: I don't care! You must tell me everything.

Holmes: Very well, I will be brief. Vampirism is not the only reason that causes one to suck blood from a wound. Another is to draw off poison.

Ferguson: Poison! What poison?

Holmes: These weapons on the walls, Mr Ferguson, are those used by the pygmies of Central America. They are usually tipped with curare.

Ferguson: (in disbelief) Are you saying that someone stuck a dart, or an arrow, into the neck of my baby? That my wife knew, and tried to suck out the poison?

Holmes: Exactly.

Ferguson: Who did this?

Holmes: Someone who is jealous of your love for her. And Jealous of the baby because it is fit and strong whereas he is weak and crippled.

Ferguson: Jacky?

Holmes: As he was holding the baby just now, his back was turned to us, but I could see his reflection in the window. His face had an expression of such cruel hatred as I have seldom seen, and was quite unmistakable.

Ferguson: Jacky! I don't believe it! How could he have known those weapons were poisonous?

Holmes: Because first he tried them on the dog.

Ferguson: (aghast) Oh, my God! (to his wife) Is this true?

Marie: It is true, Roberto. I did not want to tell you because I know how you love the boy. But ... is true. I see him do it. Two times I see him.

Ferguson: (groans) Oh - what shall I do!

Holmes: Courage, Mr Ferguson. A year or two at sea will take care of Master Jacky. As for the rest - your wife is returned to you.

Ferguson: (voice breaking) My Darling ... forgive me ... please.

Marie: (tremulous) Roberto ... I love you so much ... (they embrace)

Dr Watson: (in a whisper) At this point, Holmes, I think it better if we left.

Holmes: (in a whisper) Quite so, Watson. Quite so ...

(**Scene:** the open road: ringing footsteps)

Dr Watson: Be honest with me, Holmes. You knew the answer all the time, didn't you, even before you came here.

Holmes: More or less.

Dr Watson: But how?

Holmes: Two very simple reasons. First, Ferguson told me his wife was not mad. It meant therefore, that whatever she was doing, she was doing deliberately.

Dr Watson: And the second?

Holmes: Human vampires, my dear Watson, do not exist.

My Case Notes and Glossary

The Norwood Builder

by Sir Arthur Conan Doyle
Dramatised by Michael Mandeville

Cast
Sherlock Holmes
Dr James Watson
John Hector McFarlane (a young man)
Inspector Lestrade (middle-aged)
Jonas Oldacre (aged about 50)

(**Scene:** Holmes' Rooms at 221b Baker Street, London.)
Dr Watson: (**narration**) It was just before breakfast on a morning in July, 1890, when Holmes and I, bored with life because there was no work, were disturbed by a loud knocking at the door downstairs. A moment later a young man was shown into the room.

McFarlane: (breathless and frightened) I'm sorry, Mr Holmes! Please don't blame me. I am nearly dead with worry. I am John Hector McFarlane.
Holmes: Oh, really? Please sit down. A cigarette? That's better ... Now, who on earth is John Hector McFarlane, and why does he want to see me so urgently?
McFarlane: I ...
(The door bursts open) enter Inspector Lestrade of Scotland Yard, rather officious, loud and rough)
Lestrade: Aha! There you are! John Hector McFarlane I arrest you for the murder of Jonas Oldacre!
Holmes: (aside) So that's who he is!
McFarlane: (wildly) It wasn't me! I never did it!
Lestrade: Sorry to disturb your breakfast, Mr Holmes.
Holmes: (affably) Not at all, Inspector. You're very welcome. Have a kipper.
Lestrade: Not just now.
Holmes: A cup of tea, then?
Lestrade: No, thank you. I'm a busy man, Mr Holmes, and I have my duty ...
Holmes: And Mr McFarlane is my client and I have mine. Coffee?
Lestrade: No, no ...
Holmes: Have some of this, then.
Lestrade: What is it?
Holmes: To me it's sausage - what happened to Jonas Oldacre?
Lestrade: He was murdered.

The Norwood Builder

Holmes: So I gather. What are the details?

Lestrade: (breathes hard) Very well than ... Last night this young fellow here called on Mr Jonas Oldacre at his house in Norwood - he gave his name to the housekeeper when she let him in. The two were together for a long time and so she went to bed. She was awakened just after midnight by a fire at the back of the house. Oldacre was a builder and had a stack of lumber there. She also said there was a strong smell of burning flesh, which the Fire Brigade, arriving soon afterwards, confirmed. While they were putting out the fire she went in search of her master, only to find he had disappeared. But his room was in great disorder. The safe was open and papers were scattered about. There were signs of a struggle - furniture knocked over - and a walking stick with the initials JHM was found in a corner.

McFarlane: That's mine! I was wondering where I had left it!

Lestrade: It had blood on it.

McFarlane: (gasps) What!

Holmes: Where do you live, Mr McFarlane?

McFarlane: In Blackheath, with my mother, who is a widow.

Holmes: Did you go home last night?

McFarlane: No. The last train had gone, so I stayed in an hotel near the station.

Lestrade: Very convenient ...

Holmes: But also quite possible. What did happen?

McFarlane: I don't know - It's the strangest thing. I only met Mr Oldacre for the first time yesterday. I am a solicitor you see, and about three o'clock in the afternoon he walked into my office in the City... (fade out to McFarlane's chambers)

McFarlane: ... Mr Oldacre? I don't believe I've had the pleasure.

Oldacre: (middle aged, sly) Ah, but your mother has, Mr McFarlane. She and I are very old friends.

McFarlane: Oh, er ... well, what did you want to see me about?

Oldacre: I want to make a will. I'm a rich man, but I'm getting on a bit now, and I want to make sure my money goes to the right hands. I've written out a rough draft ...

McFarlane: May I see it?

Oldacre: Of course. (sound of rustling paper)

McFarlane: (bewildered) But ... Mr Oldacre ... This will is made out to me!

Oldacre: (laughing uneasily) Yes, that's right.

McFarlane: But why?

Oldacre: Well, I'm a bachelor, you see, with no living relatives; and seeing as how I've always heard what a deserving young man you were ...

McFarlane: Well!

Oldacre: I've decided to make you my heir. Now what I want you to do is this:

prepare the will I've just given you, and bring it to my house in Norwood tonight. I have other documents there I want you to sign. But you must promise not to tell anyone about this. I want it kept a secret until everything is settled. (fade out: return to Holmes' rooms)

McFarlane: I went there as he asked, without telling anyone, but there was too much work for us to finish in one evening and so I left, just before midnight, after arranging with Mr Oldacre to return the following evening.
Holmes: How did you know about the murder?
McFarlane: I read about it in this morning's paper. That's why I came straight to you!
Holmes: Oh ...Well, never fear! I shall handle your case with pleasure.
McFarlane: Thank you so much.
Lestrade: (heavily) Well, if that's all, Mr Holmes...
Holmes: Thank you, Inspector. I won't keep you any longer.
Lestrade: Thank you.
Holmes: Not at all. Some toast before you go?
Lestrade: (rudely) Garn! (exits and the door closes)
Dr Watson: (chuckling) Poor Lestrade. He certainly doesn't like to have you mixed up in his cases. What are you going to do now?
Holmes: I think I shall start at Blackheath.
Dr Watson: Blackheath? But the murder was committed in Norwood!
Holmes: So I believe. Ask Mrs Hudson to keep some supper for me, would you?
Dr Watson: All right. Anything special?
Holmes: (vaguely) Sausage, Watson. Just sausage.

Dr Watson: (**narration**) But Holmes's pleasure at finding work, did not last. When he returned at suppertime his face was grave.
Holmes: Motive, Watson! I cannot find a motive, and the more I look the more unclear it becomes.
Dr Watson: I presume you went to Blackheath, as you said?
Holmes: I did. Mrs McFarlane, our client's mother was the person I wanted to see.
Dr Watson: Did she remember Oldacre?
Holmes: Oh yes, and to my astonishment, she hated him! Apparently he wanted to marry her once, but she would have nothing to do with him. She described him to me as "more like a cunning and malignant ape than a human being".
Dr Watson: That's pretty strong!
Holmes: But justified. She showed me a photograph of herself, cut and muti-

lated with a knife. Oldacre sent it to her like that on her wedding morning, with his curse.

Dr Watson: Dreadful! But do you think that reason enough for her son to kill him?

Holmes: I doubt it. And it certainly doesn't explain why Oldacre would want to leave him all his money.

Dr Watson: What did you do after that?

Holmes: I went to Norwood. It's a big, new, ugly house, designed and built by Oldacre himself. I spoke to the housekeeper - whom I did not trust, and who, I am certain, knows far more than she is prepared to say. I had a look at the fire, where the police had found some pieces of burned cloth and some buttons from one of Oldacre's jackets, together with some charred bones, and I went over the house from top to bottom but I could find nothing either to prove or disprove McFarlane's story.

Dr Watson: Did you look through the papers he talked about?

Holmes: Yes. There were a lot of letters from creditors, and records of several large cheques, made out to a Mr Cornelius and drawn on a bank in Reading. Beyond that, nothing of interest and certainly no motive for murder.

Dr Watson: It's a strange business.

Holmes: It's more than strange, Watson - the whole thing is wrong. But I cannot see where. No - no supper, thank you. An ounce of good tobacco, and my violin. Just leave me alone - I have to think. (wailing violin in background)

Dr Watson: (narration) I went to sleep with the sound of Holmes' violin in my ears. When I awoke in the morning he was still playing, and appeared to be quite as fresh as I. But then a telegram arrived, dashing his mood again.

Holmes: It's from Lestrade. He's down at Norwood. "Important new evidence discovered. McFarlane's guilt definitely established. Advise you abandon case. Lestrade."

Dr Watson: (drily) That's nice of him.

Holmes: (fiercely) I don't believe it! He can't have found anything.

Dr Watson: Let's go and see for ourselves. But we'll have some breakfast first shall we?

Holmes: Give it to the cat, Watson ... we're going to Norwood!

(**Scene:** Jonas Oldacre's house in Norwood)

Lestrade: (triumphantly) There you are, Mr Holmes - a bloodstained thumb print, down there, on the wall.

Holmes: Dear me ... Is this McFarlane's?

Lestrade: Indeed it is! I checked it myself. I always said he was guilty, and this is

final proof. I ... (change of tone) What are you laughing at?

Holmes: (trying to hide his merriment) For once, Lestrade, I think you're right. This is final!

Lestrade: Just what I said.

Holmes: Call a constable, would you, and tell him to bring some straw and a bucket of water. I'm going upstairs. (exits)

Lestrade: (bewildered) Straw? Bucket of water? What's he talking about?

Dr Watson: I've no idea, but I should do as he says.

Lestrade: Lot of nonsense. I dunno. (calling) Constable! (fade out to upstairs corridor)

Lestrade: (heavily) All right, Mr Holmes - here's your 'straw'. What do you want done with it?

Holmes: Just put it on the floor at the end of this passage (rustling of straw) That's right. Now, I'll Just set light to it ... (sounds appropriate) Good - lots of smoke (they all begin coughing) Ready? All together: (he begins shouting) Fire! Fire!

Dr Watson: (joining in) Fire! Help! Fire!

Lestrade: What on earth ...?

Holmes: Come on, Lestrade - and you, Constable: Shout – Fire! Fire!

Constable: Fire! Fire!

Lestrade: Have you all gone mad?

Dr Watson: Look! There's a door opening in the wall at the end!

Lestrade: My God! There's someone coming out!

Dr Watson: Who is it?

(sound of coughing)

Lestrade: Who are you?

Holmes: Let me introduce you, Lestrade. This is Mr Jonas Oldacre.

Lestrade: What?

Oldacre: (whining) It was all a joke, sir, a practical joke. I meant no harm by it, I do assure you.

Lestrade: You're Jonas Oldacre?

Oldacre: Yes, Indeed, sir.

Lestrade: And you've been hiding in that secret room all the time?

Oldacre: Only a joke, sir, as I explained.

Lestrade: (wrathfully) You horrible little man. You nearly got someone hanged for murder.

Oldacre: Oh, really now.

Lestrade: Constable -Take him away.

Constable: Right, sir.

Oldacre: Wait - I can explain everything!

Constable: Come along, you.

Oldacre: Oh! Oh! (footsteps recede)

Lestrade: (at a loss) Well, Mr Holmes, I really don't know what to say. I, er ... But how did you know? I don't understand.

Holmes: The thumb-print on the wall, Lestrade. When I examine a place, I examine it. That thumb-print was not there yesterday, therefore it must have been placed there overnight. It couldn't have been McFarlane because he's in gaol therefore it must have been Oldacre.

Lestrade: (amazed) How did he do it?

Holmes: McFarland came here to sign documents, didn't he? How do you do that? By putting your thumb onto a piece of wax. It was quite easy for Oldacre, later, to transfer the wax impression to the wall, using some of his own blood.

Lestrade: But why?

Holmes: (grimly) Motive, Lestrade. Find the motive and you've found your man. Oldacre hated McFarlane's mother - did you know that?

Lestrade: No!

Holmes: You should have. Revenge is a powerful reason. Oldacre was also in debt - did you know that?

Lestrade: No, I confess I didn't.

Holmes: That is another reason to disappear. Oldacre decided to combine the two.

Lestrade: I was right about one thing. He certainly is a horrible piece of work How did you know where to find him?

Holmes: I measured the house.

Lestrade: What was the smell of burning flesh?

Holmes: A dead dog, I should think.

Lestrade: And the housekeeper?

Holmes: An accomplice. Arrest her.

Lestrade: Where was he going, after he disappeared?

Holmes: Reading, probably.

Lestrade: Under what name?

Holmes: Cornelius.

Lestrade: You drink, do you, Mr Holmes?

Holmes: Whisky and soda.

Lestrade: You must allow me to buy you one.

Holmes: Make it two.

Lestrade: (laughing) You certainly have all the answers! (Holmes' laughter joins his: fade out)

Dr Watson: (**narration**) For the record: John Hector McFarlane was released from prison and Jonas Oldacre took his place. He was later charged with Attempted Murder and sentenced to five years' imprisonment with hard labour. There are no details of the trial, however,
as Sherlock Holmes said at the time, "It's all sausages to me, Watson". I really don't know where he gets some of his expressions...

My Case Notes and Glossary

www.ingramcontent.com/pod-product-compliance
Lightning Source LLC
Chambersburg PA
CBHW071738020426
42331CB00008B/2090